Life Within His Promises

By Sherrie Brown

*"You hold treasures of wisdom
more valuable than gold,*

*and we hold testimonies of Your greatness
the world needs to hear."*

I dedicate my book 'Life Within His Promises' to my Lord Jesus Christ, who is my Rock and to my wonderful family for their support.

I thank my spiritual parents and mentors Pastor Frank and Kathy, who opened their lives to me 32 years ago and poured out their love, imparting wisdom, and direction, and have continued to support me throughout my life.

Table of Contents

Testimonies

Sherrie hears from the Lord and receives beautiful heavenly prayers, which will resonate in my heart each time I read them.

It is noticeable; the Holy Spirit directs her with her prayers, as they're filled with the power of Jesus Christ.

The words penned hold powerful and meaningful prayers; leaving me feeling the mountains in my life will move after I read them

Steve Chittenden / Senior Advancement Director / China Ministry Director for Multiplication Network Ministries

"Sherrie's words have always left me feeling more of God's presence. Her prayers have always felt as though I am reading through Psalms. I'm grateful for the impact her prayers have had on my soul. She would send me one of her prayers, and it would be exactly what my heart needed; a heavenly perspective with faith to believe.

Sue Piatt-Side by Side Studios

"The prayers, Sherrie has written, have offered me hope and peace. They bring forth truth and light to my position in Jesus and His character and nature toward me. Her writings read like a devotional, or daily prayer book, which helps build up my faith and trust in the Lord."

Rhiannon Staal

We have been able to apply her God ordained, prayers and prophetic insights into the heart of God immediately. Her gift has helped develop a boldness in us that has allowed us to reach out to others, even more, with the love of Jesus.

Pastor Jon Youngquist

Sherrie truly walks in signs, wonders and miracles as the word of God speaks of.

Sherrie has an amazing connection with the Lord; receiving powerful messages, visions, and prophecies.

I have grown in my faith just by reading her God-given prayers.

I believe your spirit will be stirred and encouraged as mine has been.

Esther O'Reilly-Massage Therapist

God powerfully uses Sherrie, communicating the Father's heart to His children.

Poetic in nature, these God-breathed prayers are love letters from Heaven.

I love the way she relays the Lord's promises; instantly quieting my soul, restoring faith and summoning my Spirit man to rise and be the warrior Christ calls me to be.

She is gifted prayers bring joy, hope, peace, and freedom and are reminders of His majesty and faithfulness in our daily lives.

Lea Hayward

Introduction

1 Samuel 17:48 (NIV) "David quickly ran toward the battle line to meet Goliath."

While armored soldiers fled, David, full of bold courage, moved toward the danger Goliath represented.

He knew he had the backing of heaven, and with confidence and faith, David took out Goliath with a stick and a stone.

I have learned, when faith manifests, it rises up and pushes back; boldly standing up to fear-fueled intimidation, and its destruction.

Over the years, when I've faced fear, it has tried to dominate my emotions, while my faith seemingly shrinks losing it rightful, God-given place in my spirit.

"Faith bows to the fear-filled occupant,
for it seeks quiet trust, in the place of bold fear."

Bill Johnson

Faith doesn't get in our face, insisting we react; it merely comes because we called and stays because we asked.

Peace waits in Gods secret place, within His Holy Spirit, where fear holds no ground, and victory is assured.

If there is something I would be doing, if I were not in fear, I have allowed fears ferocious roar to determine my destiny and not Jesus.

You will find a theme in this book, given divinely by the Lord.

Within its pages, you will read powerful declarations and Scriptures, woven throughout.

THE GOODNESS
OF GOD IS ETERNAL

You carry Your beloved safely, lifting and delivering us to our anticipated dwelling, inhabiting Your liberty releasing us to freedom. Our hearts sing a new song, a victorious sound, and a battle cry! Swing wide, You heavenly gates; we long to plant our flags of victory declaring, "*It is well with my soul!*".

My Heart Sings a new Song

L ord, each day we choose to step into our destiny. Your map of our lives was laid out before time began.

You hold treasures of wisdom more valuable than gold, and we hold testimonies of Your greatness the world needs to hear.

Within the bounds of this arranged journey, we meet face to face with You, Lord. Your provision is in its perfect place for each moment of our day.

At times our soul begs and pleads, for its own way, but Your voice beckons us to deeper waters, where faith is required.

We've carried within our soul, a vast sea of pain and disappointments, begging for an impartation of Your healing touch, Lord. You tenderly breach the walls, we unknowingly erect around our heart, gaining access in; creating beauty for ashes.

Your desire, Lord, is to cause those places, to become fruitful vines with Your elaborate fullness and Your healing love. We yearn for You to occupy the unfamiliar places where restoration has yet to arrive.

You patiently wait, standing by, while we wrestle the strongholds of generations before, teaching us how to fight and win. We've kept our distance at times and made a stand against Your invitation, but Your conquering love tarries and wins every time.

You cannot heal the brokenness within our souls, without our permission, and we know You yearn to guide us in; moving Your children through the Valleys of Baca.

Our souls cry out, and tears are shed, languishing for Your unfailing love.

Lord, You've turned our mourning into joy, washing our inmost place, which once held secrets, with Your grace and truth. Thank You, Jesus, for being the gentleman that You are, holding open the door, ushering us through the fires and floods; and into our promised land.

You carry Your beloved safely, lifting and delivering us to our anticipated dwelling, inhabiting Your liberty releasing us to freedom. Our hearts sing a new song, a victorious sound, and a battle cry! Swing wide, You heavenly gates; we long to plant our flags of victory declaring, "*It is well with my soul!*"

Psalm 24:7-9

Psalm 46:1-3

Psalm 51:6

Psalm 84:6

Isaiah 27:2

Psalm 91:1

You are GOOD News

L ord Jesus, You are the Good News; therefore, there is NO bad news! Your goodness goes before us and surrounds us as a shield! Being our rear guard assures us a secure path, one that the enemy cannot follow.

We are empowered daily, immersed in Your living water, cleansing us

from our past. This washing enables us to see more clearly the ways of Your kingdom power!

Your will for us is that we bring Your kingdom into our world, and display a victorious life, one that is overshadowed by You. Call us servants, Lord, bond slaves like Paul, for he knew his life was not his own.

May Your word leap off the pages as we read them, and into our readied hearts. Purify us, create in each of us clean hearts, and renew within a right spirit. Each day we'll make Your word our prayers and live out its pages; our map to freedom.

You declare, "*My Kingdom come, My will be done, on earth as it is in heaven.*" Your glorious power is waiting to be displayed throughout the world, yet how can it be if we're not willing!

We offer ourselves as instruments for You to play, giving heavenly sweet music to an increasingly deaf world. We will align ourselves with You, our conductor, who longs to bring the sound of heaven to earth.

Pick us up, Lord and cradle us, while You strike our cords, ushering in heavenly notes to a world who's lost Your rhythm. May we be heavenly harps, and while playing us, You'll pull back the earthly noise, and swallow up the places that are void of You. Play a new song Lord, one that displaces the angry and vicious voices that seem louder each day!

Each time we meet, You'll see us yielding, to Your placement, while You arrange a heavenly choir. Your eyes move to and fro, seeking willing children, eager to have You as their Conductor. Lord, You are the Composer, and Author of our lives.

I pray the words, in the song You write of us, reflect a portion if not all our lives. While You sing these songs You write, may they say, "*They trusted me, and overcame the world that was against them.*"

Psalm 3:3

Psalm 18:35

Psalm 40:3

Psalm 42:10

Psalm 96:1

Psalm 108:2

Isaiah 58:8

Limitless God!

The Lord spoke to my heart, "*I am LIMITLESS!*" I responded, "You ARE the LIMITLESS God, the God of wonders and a God of thunder. With one touch of Your mighty hand, You bring restraint to lawlessness, and freedom to those shackled by fear".

Lord, You know no boundaries, for You created the endless seas and our infinite universe. We recognize You, Lord, in the heavens above, where wars rage and battles are won.

We "Stand" in awe of Your invisible victories, ones that our eyes cannot see. We are able to "Stand" triumphant, for You let us know, You're fighting for us.

We "Stand' confident, because You sent Your word, Who became flesh; His name is Jesus, and He dwells among us. As we enter into Your presence, we feel confident determination, because Your word gives an invitation to "*Be brave and you will see the Lord save you today.*" (Exodus 14:13 CEV).

We shall not be moved, from our place next to You; we are resolute and securely positioned, steadfast and immovable, on the ROCK of our Salvation.

As we lean into Your right side, we feel the strength of Your strong arm and mighty power! Even in the darkest of days, You've set a place for us in the presence of our enemies. We watch You crush the plans of our adversary, and we respond with joyful singing, praising You, Lord, singing hallelujah!!

Grateful we come, and thankful we will remain; knowing we are hemmed in and protected on EVERY side! May You find us, Your children, "Standing," and not fighting battles that are not ours!

Let us be strengthened in our resolve to step forth, into greater places when we hear You summon us. You signal the way, as You forge ahead, declaring, "This is the way, My beloved children, walk in it and make Your unwavering STAND!" We will find rest when we accept as fact, the battle is Yours, the victory is ours; we win!!"

2 Samuel 22:38

2 Chronicles 20:15

Psalm 23:5

Psalm 30:21

Psalm 46:7

Psalm 46:10

Psalm 89:26

Psalm 139:5

Acts 2:25

Unstoppable God!

Lord Jesus, You are our supernatural, unstoppable, undeniable, and unbelievable Force!! We choose You as Lord and King; stepping away from the sometimes-unfruitful management of our day!

You oppose the darkness and emanate through us, as we set our faces toward the heavens, in an unbreakable stance! The things which are seen in this temporal world cause despair in the fretful, but for us who've cast our eyes on Your unseen world, hope is released.

Through faith, we'll have unbroken unity with Your invisible world, allowing Your Holy Spirit to permeate peace in ours! Let our desires which sometimes overshadow Yours, be laid at the foot of Your cross.

Your eyes search for those, whose hearts are abandoned to You; therefore, with trust, we're released into Your care. We're confident we've left ourselves with the Inventor of true love and Restorer of all that is broken!"

Troubles crumble, and darkness departs when we make our immovable stand against them!

Knowing whose we are, and what exists within our mortal bodies, we're transformed and empowered, backed by heaven filled with faith! David faced Goliath with no armor and killed him with a rock. What armored soldiers fled from, David faced, for he knew You, Lord!

Joseph faced impossibilities, imprisonment, and was seemingly cut off from his future, but You unlocked doors, created ways, gave favor and established his future!

Moses obeyed You, and the seas parted for his people, while assignments of death were chasing them. Lord, we willingly step into our futures; containing Your superpowers, back by heaven.

May You find us resolute, and unwavering in faith, giving You permission to transport us to our destinies, that hold giant impossibilities, bending their knee to the name of Jesus!

2 Chronicles 16:9

1 Samuel 17:45

Jeremiah 31:17

Jeremiah 29:11

Genesis 41:42

Exodus 14:13

Proverbs 23:18

Philippians 1:6

An always-present Lord!

Lord, may we continually recognize You, while You stand behind, before, and alongside us. Bring comfort to our soul, reminding us there's never been a time we weren't on Your mind.

We are ever reaching, toward the life You promised; the exceeding abundance and fullness within Your kingdom. For those us of who've chosen the narrow road, it appears rockier, with turns and twists; knocking us back on our heels at times.

You've given us hinds' feet, enabling our ascension toward Your summons, calling us to higher places in Your kingdom. You still the waters, and calm the storms, allowing us time to navigate the turbulent, and violent, fierce seas of fear and doubt.

The more we trust in Your flawless, unwavering love, we encounter Your peace, while shrouded by Your word. You teach us how to shut out the unrelenting, tormenting thoughts bombarding our minds, and anchor in the safe harbor with still waters of Your Spirit!

We'll not look at what we see, for we know it's temporal; therefore, we'll join with You, immersing ourselves in Your unseen realm, which holds eternal treasures.

May we unfold Your invitation; finding heavenly wisdom, ushering us to more prosperous, and fertile ground; taking us further into Your heart. Lord, I pray we find ourselves occupying our new territory, within our minds.

May we continually recall moments with You; driving out the enemies attempts to steal the conciliation You've imparted. Deep is calling us unto itself, where our thoughts find rest and our spirits are refreshed in the quietness of Your trust!

2 Samuel 22:34

Isaiah 32:17

Psalm 94:19

Psalm 42:7

John 16:33

2 Corinthians 4:18

2 Peter 1:12

Author of our lives!

Lord Jesus, this day, like every day is made for us Your children. How we live out our day and close its chapter at its end, is up to us. We acknowledge You, Lord, as the Author and Writer of our lives, and within the pages You've composed, You've ushered in liberty and freedom!

Lord, cause the fire within our souls to turn from a kindle to a flame. Breathe on us, Jesus and with the wind of Your Spirit, may we feel compelled to bend beneath, that we may rise above in power.

Let the darkness that insists on invading our lives be dispelled by the mere thought of You. As we open our mouths to speak, let the words from our lips bring forth love and freedom to the hearer.

If we shout, may the declarations be that which is penned in Your word, bringing forth life, assurance and Your message of hope. Lord, we pray that when You lead, we will follow and when we follow, You'll fiercely guard us.

The higher ground You're leading us to, promises increasing power in weakness, and living water when we thirst. May we decree, while we take this trek to attain higher ground, "We are the victors, He is our Savior, we are His children, He is our destiny!"

May we be the tips of Your sword, the strings in Your harp, the jewels in Your crown and the aroma flooding

Your throne room. We long to bring Your will, on earth, as it is in heaven.

We kneel at Your footstool, Lord and learn of You, for true humility is imparted when we yield to our Maker. As we bow before You in true weakness, may You find Your servants willing to lose our lives for Your sake.

As we are lost in You, we'll find our way, for no child of Yours has EVER died that hasn't risen again! We shall rise to greater heights and take the authority You've handed us, for now is the time and today is our day to display Your Glory!

Isaiah 55:9

Isaiah 66:1

Psalm 138:2

Matthew 10:39

2 Timothy 1:6

Your matchless power!

W e want to climb higher, go deeper, finding more of You and less of ourselves. We long to ascend our mountains of difficulty and place our banners of victory, signifying our advancement.

There is no mountain too high, or valley with deaths shadow, that You haven't already subdued. We desire to till the soil, of the ground we've found ourselves standing, bringing up the treasures from within Your word that release freedom.

Your matchless power at our side; Your unrelenting love guiding us to the parched and barren lands releasing Your words of life. As we enter in, we'll announce the Good News to those who are in great need, of freedom's touch.

Chains are broken, and captives; released from their prisons of guilt and shame, when we mention Your name, Jesus. Provision for victory lay waiting within, for You've never called us to a place where the enemy wasn't conquered.

May we get out of the boat of complacency, stepping over the edge and onto the waters, where faith is required.

You are the King of Glory, who parts the seas of doubt and takes us across to our PROMISED LAND.

Deuteronomy 33:12

Joshua 14:9

Titus 2:14

Romans 3:24

Galatians 5:1

Hebrews 11:9

Revelation 1:5

Your Pledge of Love

Your great love has no restraints, and the waters of Your refreshing Spirit, release us from our often-weary, troubled heart. We cannot outrun, Your loving kindness, or outclimb the higher heights of Your endless pursuit.

Your persistent and unrelenting love welcomes us along its side and guides us through the darkness. When the chattering voices in our minds, infiltrate, bringing fear, You remind us; You complete us, and our sufficiency is in You.

When we sink back, resting and immersed in Your love, we're bathed in Your increasing presence. You never fade away or turn away from Your beloved; instead, You steal us away, to spend time alone with You.

Your word is inscribed on the tablets of our hearts, Lord, enabling Your assurance to impart rest; capturing our hearts. All that You are, and all that You've done for us is stored in the bank of our memories!

Each time our soul is troubled, we'll make a withdrawal from our life giving, peacemaking, bank of Your power!

Infuse us, Lord, with Your fresh fire, and deep affection. May we be like David, who hid in a cave, finding refuge from his attackers. Find us unwavering in faith, not running from Your unrelenting pursuit, allowing You to overtake us, on days of despondency, with Your pledge of love.

Mark 6:31

2 Corinthians 3:3

2 Corinthians 12:9

Psalm 91:1

Psalm 119:159

You're my first thought, Lord!

The day begins, sometimes without us, but never without You Lord. You're our first thought, upon opening our eyes, and my last one as they close to sleep.

Your songs of deliverance swirl, around us, as we enter into our day. When we open the door to leave our dwelling, You open Your gates of praise, leading us into Yours.

Each day You offer new songs and promising words, that carry us through with joy.

We lift our eyes to the hills and acknowledge where our help comes from. Your word declares: "Heaven is Yours, and the earth You've given to all humanity."

You've equipped us with what is required, living out a surrendered life. We speak to the mighty mountains in our season of battles, declaring by faith, "In Jesus' Name, move aside."

What appears impossible will bow down at the mention of Your name and melt like wax, while we walk through. Stepping out in faith, not yet seeing, but still believing, we'll watch the melting of conflicts and our struggles subdued and crushed.

Trust leads us in, and whispers in our ear; letting us know we are safe, bringing us along while leaning into You.

Lord, You call us out into deeper waters of faith, leaving the shores of apprehension.

We'll beam as we step away, from the tide lines of safety, carrying courage and hope.

When clouds of adversities storm, build, bellowing loudly, we're reminded: our spirits left willingly, and we'll not submit to emotions carrying distrust and doubt.

May You consistently find us in clothed in meekness, carrying lowliness, learning from the Author of our faith, and Refuge in life's storms.

Keep holding us tight, Lord, reminding us we are never alone if we feel abandoned, and You're a breath away when we're weary. As we taste and see You, abiding in Your goodness, we'll ascend to the pinnacle of Your authority and soar on faiths wings.

Isaiah 4:6

Isaiah 32:2

Psalm 32:7

Psalm 34:8

Psalm 42:7-8

Psalm 115:16

Psalm 119:114

Proverbs 18:10

Proverbs 28:6

Proverbs 28:18

Who we are in Jesus

Each day, when entering into our day, we choose to be thankful; celebrating all that You are, and who we are in You! You were before there was time and You continue to be our beginning and our end. May we be an offering daily, surrendering our lives, grafted in to Your plans, melded into You. How can we be anything for You, if we don't get out of the way of ourselves?

We step aside, step down, and stand down, so that You may step in, step up, and stand over us. You long to overtake us with Your love; having Your way, that You may display Your capable, unquestionable power daily.

When will we yield our lives, ending the vain attempts to build on sinking sand? When will we submit to Your irreproachable influence, so that Your plans can begin? You stand and wait at the door of our decisions, desiring to be the plan we submit to!

The enemy lay waiting, ready to launch toward us, with intimidating power, interrupting the courses of our future.

Your unceasing love and undeniable peace invade our soul, when we step off the treadmill of turbulent doubt. You beckon us to Your assurance: the flawless sanctuary of unending stillness. Hurry isn't a word You created, for You don't push us to attain Your way. Your songs of deliverance, encircle us, shaping paths, and constructing inroads, if there appears to be none.

Lord, You are the Salvager of lives, arranging the best to come forth, if we only see the worst. When our world seems defeated, You unfold a map revealing we've veered off course and You're guiding us back to places where triumphal victories lie waiting.

Lead on, sweet Savior, Author, and Finisher of the plans laid before us! We're listening to You, Lord; our ears inclined, placed to Your lips, and eyes keenly aware of Your finger pointing out toward our trail we're to blaze with Your glory and fire!

We are eager to do Your will, trusting in Your unfailing love! You created us, and we long to mirror back the love You daily clothe us in. While walking among us Lord, may You find we've lost ourselves in You, yielded to and unresisting Your overwhelming love.

Ecclesiastes 3:11

Isaiah 46:10

Psalm 33:5

Psalm 62:12

Psalm 138:2

Galatians 2:20

Mark 10:28

Isaiah 64:8

Psalms 148:8

Revelations 22:13

Step into My Love

L   ord, You call us to release, let go, give up, and give
    in to Your divine plan. To step into Your will for
    our lives, one that we cannot see, which holds
countless miracles and unexplored territory for us to settle
in.

We end up, exhausting ourselves with our own resources,
while You stand tarrying, believing we will come to You.
Worry and fret seem to be the meal of the day, when
alarm and restlessness invade our soul.

You remind us, we are to live on the bread of Your word,
as our daily meal, not eating of the poisonous fruit of fear,
leading us to control. We scurry around in our minds and
bodies, anxiously attempting to eliminate trouble, instead
of pulling up the covers of peace and rest.

You gently remind us to be still, and know that You are
God, remaining in Your tight grip. We move to and fro,
from place to place, urgently pleading with You to do
something, anything, to deliver.

You quietly stand by, watching as we run out of our
options, waiting for us to lay our concerns at Your feet.
You long for Your children to surrender, letting go of the
reins of our feeble attempts to lead ourselves to an
outcome of victory.

You watch as we frantically arrange the details in our
lives, trying to prevent the death of our dreams, unwilling

to yield to Yours. "*Forgive us, Lord*," we cry out; only to begin the next day again, determined to persist on the perpetual treadmill of anxiety.

May we relinquish our lives to a Man we cannot see, to the King of the universe we cannot audibly hear. As we sink into the depths of Your heart, to the very core of Your flawless love, we will find the rest we insatiably hunger for.

We will remain thankful, as we find our way out of the unlocked prison we've created, and into the secure chambers of Your unending love.

Zechariah 9:12

Isaiah 35:4

Psalm 25:1-7

Psalm 31:2-3

Psalm 49:12

Psalm 71:2

2 Timothy 4:18

Next to You, Lord!

The Lord spoke "*I want My children to know they are a weapon, and when walking in a room, the darkness is ushered out, and My Angels are ushered in.*"

He then asked, "*Do You want to carry a weapon, or be a weapon?*"

"*I want to be a weapon of Your perfect love that casts out fear,*" I responded.

He went on to say, "*The world needs courageous leaders; those who know Me, must be bold and perfected in love. With courage, boldness, and fierce tenacity, My children must make a stand for me.*"

We declare Lord, we'll stand boldly for the advancement of Your kingdom, and wear a badge of honor; planting flags of victory in places once uninhabited. We lay hold of Your Spirit's sword and carve our names by faith in history.

May we be courageous children, with our oil lamps full, every yolk lifted, for Your anointing promises to shatter it. You are looking for those willing; therefore, we consent to all Your plans, leaving ours behind.

May You find us hiding under the shelter of Your wings and leaning into Your faithfulness. Our hearts filled with compassion will not hide in fear, but rise in faith, drawing from You all, all we'll ever need. Surrendering our lives daily to Your power from on high, we shall let praise rise from within our souls.

We desire to be likened to Esther, who allowed herself to be prepared by attendants, waiting as they imparted what was needed to meet the king. Esther's contrite heart, before her king, changed his heart; therefore, we come before You, Lord, humble, eager, and submitting to the process we're in.

The king said to Esther, *"All I have is Yours, even to the half of my kingdom."*

You let us know, *"All of my Kingdom is Yours, taste and see that I Am good!"*

We are empowered, knowing we have the backing of Your dunamis power, as we call on heaven to rain down. May we take our rightful place alongside You, Jesus, entering into places marked with danger, crushing the enemy with Your dominant and mighty love.

1 Chronicles 28:20

Psalm 27:1

1 John 4:18

John 14:27

Ephesians 6:10

You're my Anchor, Lord

L ord, You are the Anchor to our souls, and a sail on stormy days. You're the Quencher of our thirst and light up all our ways.

You're the Healer for disease, which makes all sickness flee, and You've unlocked prison cells and thrown away the keys.

You're the Builder of all bridges and restore the ancient days. You spoke one word, the earth was formed, and taught us what to say.

You're the Wind beneath our wings and ground beneath our feet, and the Victor in all battles, and our foes You'll always beat.

You're the Friend when we're without, and the pointer of our way, and the funds in our accounts and true riches are our pay.

You're the Giver of all life and the Lifter of our heads, and the One who makes us whole, and we'll follow where You've led.

You're Beginning for all ends, and the First when we are last. You'll lay the days before us and forget about our past.

You're the Opener of doors, and Light within the room, the Writer of our songs, and we love You to the moon.

You're the peace that clothes our minds, and our shade on sunny days. the answer to all questions, revealing secrets where they lay.

You're the victory before us, as Your angels march ahead, they're bringing all our promises, just like Your word has said. We love that You're transforming us, we're learning all Your ways and we'll love You till our days are gone, oh God of ancient days!

The chariot will sweetly swing, this day of which we'll see. It's coming' for to carry us home, much like the song!

Isaiah 43:18

Isaiah 61:4

Psalms 98:1

Hebrew 1:4

Hebrew 6:19

Grateful and Thankful!

L ord Jesus, we are grateful; yes, thankful and exceedingly blessed to know we have another day with You. You are the Giver of life, the Opener of all gates leading out of our wildness and into our promises. We call upon Your name, the only Name that changes lives, prevents destruction; while unlocking doors and creating out of dust.

We submit to You, the Author of our lives and the Restorer of our lost goods. If we find ourselves ahead of You, may we step aside, allowing You to lead.

Forgive us, Lord, for thinking we knew where we were headed, and the time we'd arrive. With pride seemingly pushing us, and even taking over our lives, You end up in the back seat, second place, and runner-up.

Lord, we repent for not following where You lead, nor letting You drive. We end up gripping the steering wheel of our lives and tenaciously holding tight, not surrendering the course we've set our future on.

The beauty You promise in place of ashes, is what we long for, and yet we take detours, distancing ourselves from Your will. You want to fill our lives with abundant blessings, replacing our uneasy, restless souls' weight.

At times Lord, we destroy, with our words, the very thing You bring to release freedom. You wait, desiring to step into our day, and show the way through the deep valleys of darkness, and on to our destiny.

There are times You arrive as a guest to our home, and desire to stay a lifetime, and yet we quickly usher You to the door before the visit is over. Forgive us, Lord, please remain and linger a while longer for we thirst for Your message of hope.

May we be Your vessels who carry out Your will to the brokenhearted and downcast in our midst. Stay with us, and share the much-needed words of life, Jesus, reminding us, we are to bring encouragement to the despondent in our community.

Impart all that is needed, to cause Your light to impregnate us, displaying Your wondrous love and undeniable peace!

Psalm 31:24

Psalm 95:2

Psalm 100:4

Psalm 119:37

John 1:4

Philippians 2:15

Philippians 4:6

2 Corinthians 4:15

Colossians 1:27

1 Timothy 4:4

Quiet Trust!

L ord Jesus, You invite us to come quietly and rest in Your trust. We're welcomed into Your powerful embrace, one that lets us know we are safe and secure in our unbroken unity in You.

When fear makes its entrance to terrorize, we're reminded, our foundation is in You; we only need to believe in Your infallible word. When anxiety tries breaking in, it will have no voice; its intimidation cannot move us from perfect love abiding within.

Our adversary brings threats, often saying, "Get out, stand back, move aside and let me thru!"

Faith says, "Enter in, beloved, move toward Me, stand at my side, and I'll usher You in!"

Jesus, You unceasingly call us to a deeper place, where the treasures within Your rich soil, unfold mysteries, and unmask the enemies' lies. We feel a tugging on our spirit, pulling us into Your world, requiring us to walk away from our own.

Your kingdom, glory, and power are a breath away, therefore, we set our gaze toward the heavens! You've placed Your mark upon us, and our victory is assured!

There is no place You call us to, that hasn't been prepared for our habitation. You render our enemy ineffective and harmless, positioning us to acquire our triumphal gain.

The battles waged against us were won at the Cross of Calvary, and the plans of our adversary demolished; therefore, we begin our journey into our promised land with assurance!

Line upon line, precept upon precept, from glory to glory we move through, the sometimes-hostile territory, inhabited by giants. We'll shout with a voice of triumph before we move toward our promises, placing our banners of faith in the ground, we've attained! Mercy and grace greet us, and Angels welcome us, as we enter the rich soil You've commissioned us to.

The covenant we've made with You, gives entrance to Your kingdom authority, and we'll build our fortress around it. The walls of Jericho were secured, and we'll strongly fortify our own; giving no opening for the adversary to steal what is ours.

Deuteronomy 29:12

Isaiah (NIV) 30:15

Psalm 47:5-8

Psalm 119:114

2 Corinthians 4:18

Bring us into Your fold, Lord!

We seek You, Lord, our one and only Hope for the joy we seek! Our hearts yearn for a life of freedom, imparted only by Your Holy Spirit. To be free from the dark days, purged from the relentless discouraging thoughts pounding our minds with its fury.

As we awaken each day, we quickly set our attention on You, for if our thoughts run free, we'll have a list of endless impossibilities. Capture our lives, surrendered to You, Lord, and bring us out of our directionless course. Set our feet to the pathway holding our desires, and lead us away from our own.

Bring us into Your fold, Lord, where Your capabilities expand within us, the power to accomplish Your will in our lives. In You, we find love's completeness; Your impartation, pulling us into realms of Your kingdom glory.

In the stillness of the night, we reach out, and You meet us with unceasing devotion.

We cry out in desperation, "Jesus!" thinking You're far away, only to find You standing beside us. The crushing weight of trials brings us to our knees, and even there You lie in wait for us. Without You, we have no breath, no stillness within our soul, nor faith for our dreams held within us!

Overshadow Your servants, Lord, and let Your protection and power guard our fragile souls. May Your sweet sound that resonates through heaven and earth be carried into our dwelling.

Within us lie plans unfulfilled and dreams silenced by disappointments. Unlock the places we've tarried and found no answer. Let us hear the sound of Angels breaking chains that have held us captive.

We long to bring to our world, something greater than ourselves; more tangible than what we see falling flat. Take us to the place that is higher, where fear cannot enter and Your peace welcomes all.

May You find us always eager and willing to be about Your business, for we are reminded You're daily involved in ours.

You whisper, each day, "Hush, My sweet children, don't cry, You're in my arms forever and together we will fly! We'll soar above the troubles that surround Your every day, we'll rise and enter into where My treasures daily lay!"

Deuteronomy 5:24

Psalm 29:3

Psalm 107:14

Psalm 104:1

Psalm 166:16

Acts 2:17

You search for us!

L ord Jesus, Your word declares, 2 Chronicles 16:9 CSB "For the eyes of the Lord roam throughout the earth to show himself strong for those who are wholeheartedly devoted to him"

But alas, Lord, You don't look past people who have turned away from Your love, time and again. Your great love never gives up, never stops looking, never stops waiting for the hardened hearts of those who reject You.

You long to influence those who have lost their way opening the saddened eyes of those who sleep through their pain. We devote ourselves, with affection and passion, toward Your abundance, where tenderness and mercy abound.

You said, "Taste and see that the Lord is good!" We have encountered Your goodness, Lord, and we delight to live in the land brimming with Your favor. Draw us into Your side, enabling us to reach out to those in our midst, welcoming them into the hollow of Your heart.

Let us find the strength to begin a day if we feel we're at the end of the other. Empower us, Lord, and let Your amazing grace and its sweet sound, continue to find and save us on days we feel lost.

Lord, deafen our ears to the angry voices in throngs gathered round us, who insist other gods will fulfill. May our ears and hearts, tenderly incline toward those afflicted;

listening for their faint cry for help, thru a crowd of hostility.

We that are Yours, willingly step away from the inclination to join the masses of raised voices and fear-filled declarations. Your great love thriving in us, brings hope to those without it, and faith for those who've lost it.

As we begin each day with faith and love, let the greatest be love! We will surrender to Your affections while conquering our stressful days, ushering in Your wondrous glory!

Let us build bridges of peace, over the crevasses of hostility and indifference, allowing You to restore all that was lost, creating inroads to Your heart.

2 Chronicles 16:9

Jeremiah 50:6

Psalm 69:16

Psalms 138:1

1 Peter 2:9

Ephesians 2:4

Your Spirit rises up!

I pray the Spirit of the living God rises up within, and we step into a superlative place of faith, and away from our past defeats! Let every familiar spirit that has tried chasing us down, be destroyed!

You deliver us, Lord, out of darkness, destruction, death, and depression. You set us upon You, our Rock, and then You rock our world. You rescue, redeem, restore, and daily refine us while journeying with You.

If we look over our lives and see waves of adversity, we'll also see greater waves of Your endless, provision, protection, and promises which overwhelm us.

Remind us, Lord, who we are, and that You are the greater One living in us. You remind us: no weapon formed against us shall prosper, and every tongue which rises against us in judgment, You will condemn.

Songs of deliverance are being sung over us 24/7, declaring, "Rise up, oh Spirit of the living God, magnify Yourself in Your children."

May we daily recall, we are who we SAY we are.

Your word says, "Let the redeemed of the Lord say so." We say, "We are redeemed!!"

"Let the poor say, "I am rich." We declare, "I am rich."

"Let the weak say, "I'm strong." We proclaim, "I am strong."

We confess with our lips and proclaim with our mouths, Your word, which travels before us, conquering obstacles standing in our way. We take Your words given and exercise them Lord, believing in their power.

We push back the forces of darkness because You taught us how. Your Word says, "The weapons of our warfare are not carnal, but MIGHTY to the pulling down of strongholds," therefore, we pull down strongholds of darkness and erect Your word.

We declare with our mouths, Your word, constructing our strong tower and place of refuge against our foe. We hide under Your shelter, oh Most High, and watch You battle on our behalf.

You said, "Stand and see the deliverance of Your God."

We trust in You, the God of David who slew Goliath with a rock. You'll never leave us nor forsake us. We see Your hand outstretched, extended toward us, in our direction.

May we yield to Your embrace, as You hold us so tightly, it takes our breath away, and You fill it with Your own!

Deuteronomy 33:27

2 Chronicles 20:17

1 Samuel 12:16

Isaiah 54:17

Psalm 61:3

Psalms 91:1

1 John 4:18

2 Corinthians 10:

1 Thessalonians 3:9

"Enter In," declares the Lord!

"Enter in," You declare in Your word, Lord, "into My rest, My sanctuary, My temple, My assembly, and protection." You invite us to bring along thanksgiving and praise with our hearts full of gratitude!

When we step thru Your gates of praise, we'll be approached with open arms and a smile that extends beyond Your shoulders. From a distance, while approaching, we see our beloved Savior, waiting with eagerness; compelling us to move toward Your invitation.

Will we come toward You, and not stand at the gate feeling unworthy? If we stop before entering in, You make Your way toward us, stepping over the threshold we felt unworthy to cross under. While embracing us, You press our head upon Your shoulder, feeling our weary frame giving way to Your love.

When You share Your empowering words, we feel our knees beneath begin to take hold. Once again, we are able to rise to our feet and feel Your power, enabling and infusing us with power and peace.

If we take a step back, You move toward us, assuring us, all is well, infusing us with quiet trust. You nourish our weakened hearts, now able to stand firm once again.

While gazing into our souls, thru the gates of our eyes, You see the shame give way to Your perfected love. You defend us, reminding us we are cleansed, whole, and worthy to come as we are, into Your amazing grace and abounding love.

Numbers 14:18

Psalm 86:5

Psalm 103:8

Matthew 18:3

2 Corinthians 1:21

2 Corinthians 4:7

2 Corinthians 12:8

Ephesians 1:19

Ephesians 4:7

We enter in, celebrating!

Each day, we choose to enter into Your gates, Lord, bringing adoration and thanksgiving. We visit Your courts with praise, letting You know we've entrusted our day to You.

You ask us to sing a new song, rejoicing and offering sacrifices of praise! We willingly respond to Your compelling call, for within Your word You offer a way that lifts us higher toward You.

You've set heavenly paths, before us, ones filled with possibilities. Since we are children of a risen King and all things are possible with You, we'll enter into Your new mercies You've released, reveling in their influence over our lives.

May the fullness of Your perfect gifts, continue to arrest and subdue mountains of impossibilities, Lord. You create probabilities, backed by Your power, potential and ingressive word. We'll wait in quiet trust, Lord, where strength is found, and watch You do what no man can.

Let us not be found screaming at You in frustration, to move quicker, but find us in silent meditation while You hold us in Your embrace. We desire to stay seated, beneath the shadow of Your wings, feeling only the softness of Your feathers of trust.

I pray our walk of faith is of an innocent child, who only sees their parent's arms wide open, when taking their first step. A child trusts, all obstacles are removed before them, and nothing can inhibit them from making their way forward.

May we be the same, Lord, as we move joyfully toward Your open arms of love. We hear Your voice beckoning us into deeper places where Your abundant promises and blessings never cease. Seeing Your outstretched hand offering peace, where doubt once existed, instills confidence, lighting up the darkness, which influenced and paralyzed our past.

We desire to stand in the places we fell, and hide in humility, where we once stood prideful. Hide us in the cleft of Your rock, as we submit in meekness, Lord, and elevate us to high places where our feet are secured.

We'll shout upon our arrival, "We are nothing without You, Jesus, for it is You, who brought us here to make our stand, and it is You that causes us to flourish in all things! All Praise, Honor and Glory are HIS!"

Psalm 20:5

Psalm 27:5

Psalm 47:1

Psalm 63:1

Psalm 65:5

1 Corinthians 12:31

Our future created in fullness

Lord Jesus, we thank You for paving our way, straightening the crooked roads, opening paths thru our wilderness encounters. May we enter into Your secret places which hold the mysteries of Your word.

You beckon us to the deeper places in You, Lord, where faith and trust manifest in the inward parts of our hearts. As we participate with You while navigating our sometimes-challenging days, we learn to unearth the treasures of Your spoken word, bringing up life and liberty.

While we wait, You empower, impart and impact our world, ushering in clarity and Your perfected peace! Lord, You long to bestow something great, imparting what may be missing in our lives.

When we come, hands open, arms lifted toward the heavens in complete surrender to Your will, You grin from ear to ear! Thank You, Lord, for letting us know; when we follow Your lead, You'll fiercely guard us, surrounding us with Your glory.

With You as our Defender, we'll be stirred in our hearts by perfect peace and security, knowing You have our backs!

Open up the highways of Your kingdom, Lord, and may You continue to fill our world with Your own! May we live in divine acceleration, as we maneuver thru open thresholds, which contain fresh experiences for increased faith.

Your word is firm and held together by Your integrity and flawless nature; steadily increasing within us, lengthening, adding and multiplying, sending forth Your power from on high.

Lord, You've let us know, reigning and ruling on earth as You are in heaven, is what we were created for. Forgive us, Lord for not allowing You to be Captain, setting the courses of our lives and away from drifting aimlessly.

We are Your receptacles, waiting on You for instruction, when thunder signals a storm is brewing. Your disciples woke You up while in the boat, because terror overcame them, when their senses perceived danger.

Let us be at peace, just as You were while sleeping through the raging storms, in high seas. Your dominion over the sea, caused its waves to cease, and the wind to bow in silence.

Calm filled the atmosphere, while Your authority was displayed, and the waves that once frightened Your disciples turned inward, bringing peace and infusing faith. We long to release faith and not fear, with Your power to silence the tempests circling around us.

May we choose the path of quiet trust, finding ourselves reclining in Your embrace while You whisper, "Hush child, you never have to fear; rest in Me beloved, you'll arrive safely, while trusting Me."

Psalm 27:5

Psalm 37:23

Psalm 37:24

Psalm 51:6

Psalm 81:7

Psalm 91:1

John 14:27

Mark 4:39

Each day is a gift!

Today is unlike any day because it's new and a gift from You, Lord! From the moment our eyes open in the morning, You unfold plans for us, allowing prosperity and not harm, for a future filled with blessings and hope.

Will we stop and be still, inclining our ear toward You, carrying out Your will for our lives? May we enter into Your courts with thanksgiving, bringing no complaints; for Your word lets us know, You inhabit our praises.

Your scriptures abundantly filled with stories of those who didn't stop and rest, to embrace Your blessings and provision, but wandered and lost their promised land. They were blinded by their emotions, with hardened hearts, and ears deafened, refusing to adhere to their leaders' directives.

Since the letter of the law kills, we choose You, being fully aware, following Your Holy Spirit, who assures us we triumph over the adversary!

Lord, may You find us engaged in Your supernatural plans, and not our own. Your word transports us to Your Kingdom, where advancements are being made, and when we're forceful in our pursuit of heaven's domain.

Signs, wonders, and miracles follow those of us who believe, giving us a glimpse of Your mighty power's impact over our lives and those in our midst.

When we are abiding in You, failure will never follow, for Your word gives us assurances and vows, You work ALL things for good! We feel great confidence in You, having made a pledge, letting us know You are behind us, as our rear guard!

Your word, gives us a guarantee, securing and hemming us in, as a shield around and about us. We are wonderfully secured and hedged in, behind and before, and Your word is a fortress and tower over us!

Genesis 28:15

Isaiah 27:31

Isaiah 52:12

Proverbs 30:5

Psalm 4:1

Psalm 121:8

Psalm 139:5

We choose Your life, Lord!

L ord, we step into our prophetic life, the moment we say, "I choose You." You gave an invitation into Your protection, and created the provision for every problem. You've turned all impossibilities into the possible, and imparted perseverance for the process!

There's hope, when the road we're on gets bumpy, and the load feels weighty. Before launching into this anointed path, we make sure we've packed assurance, for You let us know before we began, our way to victory has been cleared.

As we fix our eyes on the unseen, Your kingdom comes down, and Your glory fills our souls. Your promises fan the flames of faith and hope, dispersing any ploys of the enemy to hinder Your plans.

Gates are held open before us, while we move forward, declaring our gratitude for You, with thanksgiving and praise. You stand, waiting like the Gentleman that You are, not pushing or pulling, when we travel under the threshold of our promises.

Instead, You reveal trepidations, deception, which slow us down, and You point the way for us who forge on courageously. Lord, You remind Your children: supernatural bravery is waiting, to face the giants standing in our way. You remind us in Your word, You set the table before us in the presence of our enemies, and prevail over all powers waged against us!

We'll learn to have an appetite for overcoming, as You've taught us, fear grows giants and faith will demolish and conquer them! The angels that are given charge over us move out ahead, pushing back the darkness and rolling out our weapons of mass destruction.

Since one puts a thousand to flight, and two releases ten thousand, our declarative prayers thwart the works of darkness. Subduing and demolishing the adversary is what You do Lord, in Your matchless power, and the warfare around us is crushed.

You, Jesus, are the Way-maker, Hope-builder, Faith-imparter, and Darkness-dispeller! Our enemies are Yours, and they bow to Your great name! On our conquest to occupy the land we've been called to, we're assured You have secured our promise land, and trails are blazed for others to forge onward to their destiny! As we stand firmly next to You, with our hearts' eyes opened and ears inclined to You, we will not miss one thing You have to say, while You lead our way!

Joshua 1:5
Psalm 5:11
Psalm 143:9
Luke 17:21
1 Corinthians 16:13
Ephesians 6:14
Galatians 5:1
Hebrew 12:2

You summon us, Lord

L ord, You summon us daily, signaling us, to come out of complacency and distrust, and into Your supernatural world. You're the God of the impossible, illogical and unreasonable.

Your infallible word declares, "Nothing is impossible when we believe!"

Your desire is for us to reflect determination and courage, facing what looks frightful, allowing our conquering faith to rise! We lay down our inclination to feel timid, and instead, lay a foundation of courage and fortitude!

You spoke to Joshua [Joshua 1:9 (NLT)], *"This is My command – be strong and courageous! Do not be afraid or discouraged, for the Lord, Your God is with you wherever you go!"*

Four times we read in Joshua, "Do **not** fear, be **strong**, I Am with You."

Lord, You deliver us into our promises, if we find we've stopped at the door of them. Fulfillment and not failure, victory and not defeat, are in store for us when we heed to Your word. You take us to the front line of our timidity and conquer the adversary, who relentlessly tries to intimidate.

Fear reduces us, faith infuses and empowers; therefore, we confront fears, roar with tenacity and an expectant heart.

Whether the enemy is small, or we are outnumbered, we win every time!

The way to Your power and courage is thru weakness; therefore, we'll step thru the threshold of Your mighty word. We will not hesitate while entering in with firmness and fortitude, no longer exposed to the elements of the storms we face.

As hope takes us in, it stays at our side, and when we exit the valleys, that once appeared hopeless, we're empowered. Confidence is infused within us, as we are reminded; with perseverance and power, nothing can stand in our way.

You call us to lives above, and not beneath, giving us hind's feet for high places.

Though we have an adversary who prowls, making ferocious noises, we will stand our ground; not being swayed or moved off our course!

We'll raise our staffs, like Moses, and pull down Your Kingdom power, crushing the head of the enemy! We lift our voices of praise, dedicating every victory to You Lord, the One to whom **all** honor is due!!

Joshua 1:6
Daniel 2:37
Daniel 7:27
2 Samuel 22:34
Psalm 145:11
Habakkuk (KJV) 3:19
Mark 9:23
1 Corinthians 4:20

VICTORIES IN THE MIDST OF WAR

We live in a time, where fear is increasing; therefore, we must rise above, to Your lofty seat to conquer it. We are positioned, Lord, at the right hand of Your righteousness and given kingdom power; therefore, conquering fear is our daily bread.

We'll align ourselves with our King, the One who has given assurance of victory, and stand our ground. Our banners of love and courage are firmly planted, for You assured us when we invited You in, our enemy is OUT!

We shall disengage from doubt, that causes confusion, and live our lives like a branch resting in its vine. There's no struggle for a branch, drawing life while grafted into its quiet place of surrender.

In faith, there's no fear!

We live in a time, where fear is increasing; therefore, we must rise above, to Your lofty seat to conquer it. We are positioned, Lord, at the right hand of Your righteousness and given kingdom power; therefore, conquering fear is our daily bread.

We'll align ourselves with our King, the One who has given assurance of victory, and stand our ground. Our banners of love and courage are firmly planted, for You assured us when we invited You in, our enemy is OUT!

We shall disengage from doubt, that causes confusion, and live our lives like a branch resting in its vine. There's no struggle for a branch, drawing life while grafted into its quiet place of surrender.

When we know Who holds us up, in our securely fortified place, relinquishing our will to the Victor is effortless. We've been given the advantage, for You have fully readied and equipped us to conquer our foes.

This peace-filled path holds victory; therefore, there'll be no expectation of failure, despairing at what lies ahead. We will not be carriers of fear, but WARRIORS of FAITH.

Remind us of Your word, Lord, "There's no fear in love," only the unbreakable union with You, while in our valleys of darkness. May we only make room for the increase of Your Spirit, for there we shall find the calm we seek.

Your standards and banners multiply in strength, and usher in Your great grace and protection. Our senses will be acutely aware of the sounds of heaven and Your angelic hosts' battle cry. Let songs of love, and deliverance, invade our earth, amidst the sometimes deafening sounds of war.

Your strong Arm consistently hands over triumph, and our adversary is defeated; therefore, we'll run into places others flee from. We've been shown, every turn we take, our opponent loses, and Your righteousness has laid beneath our feet a path to run and not grow weary.

Pulling away what veiled our hearts, You remove obstructions preventing us from grasping Your truths. No webs of fear shall be woven; no plans of the enemy will stand! Nothing will hinder while traveling our secure path, leading into life's battles and out of fear's grip.

We rejoice in who You are, Lord, our Defender, and Victor over death. We'll make our way forward when You call, for we know we're safely hidden inside Your unwavering, shelter and steadfast love.

Isaiah 35:4

Isaiah 41:10

Isaiah 43:1

Psalm 23:4

Psalm 27:11

Matthew 6:34

John 14:27

1 Corinthian 15:55

Faith Stands!!

Faith comes and takes us by the hand, and with patience and love, guides us to our destiny. Fear arrives, like a freight train on steroids, shaking the very ground we stand on. It pushes, pulls, drags and drives us to places we were never meant to be.

Faith speaks carefully and clearly, making sure we understand and attain the peace that accompanies it.

Fear crashes in, makes a bold ferocious entrance that knocks us back on our heels, and takes our breath away! It intimidates and shouts, making demands, using its force, insisting on having its way. It acts superior, bullying and terrorizing us, causing the hearer to cower.

Faith approaches gently, acutely aware, and mindful of the one it tenderly holds to its side. It speaks with softness and clarity, making sure the listener doesn't miss a single word.

Faith doesn't get in our face, insisting we react; it simply comes because we called and stays because we asked. Fear tries to make residents, building a fortress that won't easily submit when we demand that it leave.

Faith gives us the boldness to rise up and tell fear, "Get OUT, in Jesus' Name, you are not wanted here, depart from me!" The message of faith builds hope and increases our peace.

If the thoughts I am having bring fear, the messenger is not God. If the thoughts I am having usher in peace, the messenger is Jesus. Who will I believe? Who am I letting guide me each day?

Romans 1:7

Act 3:16

2 Corinthians 1:24

Galatians 3:23

Hebrews 11:7

Isaiah 35:4

Isaiah 43:11

Peter 3:14

Faith Breaths Fresh Fire!

Fear huffs and puffs, and tries to blow our faith down. It gets in our face, puts its finger on our chests and pushes until we react!

Faith stands, knocking at the entrance to our hearts, and wraps its arms around us, bringing peace and comfort. Faith never leaves; if we ask it to stay, it remains forever when we yield to it.

Fear tries laying claim to our faith-filled victories, persuading us to come out of our place of rest that faith provides!

When we welcome faith in, the enemies of God flee! Faith and trust drive out darkness, creating a clearly lit path, to the riches of God's Kingdom. We lay claim to God's Word, which lets us know of the promises held for us along faith's road.

May we no longer surrender to the intimidating voice, that intimidation insists on using. We'll let assurance in God and trust in His word, have its residence in our heart, flooding our very soul.

With hope and assurance abiding within, we can stand through the storms and floods life holds. We shall live by faith, hope, and love, letting love be the overwhelming force that moves me each day!

Habakkuk 2:4

Hebrews 10:38

Galatians 3:11

2 Corinthians 5:7

Romans 1:17

Faith Dominates!

Where fear dominates, faith yields and shrinks. Faith bows to the fear-filled occupant, for it seeks quiet trust, in the place of bold fear. When faith manifests, it rises up and pushes back, boldly standing up to fear-fueled intimidation, causing its destruction.

Anxiety and terror are tenants trying to claim rights to the property it thinks it holds. Faith with courage is the landlord when we become believers, and faith must be exercised.

As children of God, we must invite faith in, and give it a key, creating its place of residency. As faith moves in and sets up its home within us, we must make sure to never give away faith's key, and give it to fear.

Faith needs a partner to come alongside and help cultivate its habitation. As faith moves past doubt and distrust, it is enlarged; remaining active and alive, it is taking over every room of the residence it moves into. Anxiety and worry will no longer have a place to enter when we allow faith to quietly and courageously stand guard at the threshold of our minds.

If fear comes knocking, faith will quickly answer, giving a swift summation as to why it will never be allowed in. The power of our words, backed by faith's promises, is enough to thwart fear's attempt to gain access to our thoughts.

God's word, active and alive within us, will consistently dominate when we let it have the lead. Faith will be protected and upheld as our legal occupant when we terminate the agreement we made with fear.

We will write over the doorposts of our minds and hearts, *"Faith, hope and love reside here – and the greatest of these is love!"*

Isaiah 35:4

Isaiah 41:10

Isaiah 43:1

Habakkuk 2:4

Haggai 2:5

Galatians 3:11

Hebrews 10:38

Standing against the darkness

In a day of the rise of fear, we'll be like Abraham who did not waiver in his faith, but grew stronger over time. We'll not give way to the adversary's intimidation with his raucous roars, creating fear.

We will lengthen our stakes of victory that we've driven in the ground, displaying Your love, securing our territory. Our confidence is bolstered, knowing You stand behind Your impenetrable word.

We'll live hidden under Your strong tower; although this place seems dark at times, we feel secure by Your side. We'll not agree with doubt, nor will we be pulled into a pit of lies; but only make a stalwart stand for our King.

We are positioned under Your authority, acknowledging Your great power! With our sight set on Your kingdom values, our riches glorify Your supernatural world, not our own.

We smell the sweet aroma of Your throne room, pouring over us, and the fragrance flowing from heaven's floor, filling the gates of these temples. Quiet trust is our restful place, one that is impassable to the darkness.

The enemy may rush toward us, hoping we'll recoil, but we've made an unmovable stance, one that will not be broken. You have secured a place within Your heart, Lord, its invisible and untraceable to the enemy.

While making our home in Your supernatural world, may we lean into Your strength and not our own, having faith in the One who called us out of darkness into a wondrous light!

Proverbs 18:10

Isaiah 54:2

Psalms 32:8

John 12:3

Romans 4:20

2 Corinthians 2:14-15

1 Peter 2:9

Endless trust in You, Lord

F reedom is felt, Lord, when we fight the "Good" fight of faith. It is our endless trust in You that causes our hope to soar and increase our faith. As we overcome discouraging days, feeling pressed on every side, we step up and in, intentional in our pursuit of You, Lord.

Encouraged by Your word, knowing there are heights in Your kingdom to attain, we ask You to point us toward our heavenly staircase, ascending toward Your majesty! Only peace awaits in this secret place, where fear holds no ground, and victory is assured.

Our help comes from You, Lord, and though we don't audibly hear Your voice, we follow Your word which displays an express way to our victory!

The tablets of our hearts are inscribed with Your wondrous word; therefore, our paths to liberty and freedom are confirmed! We hear heaven's floor rumble, and see Your great signs thundering in the skies above!

The earth is Your footstool, and we, Your children, sit eagerly at Your feet, mentioning Your name to passers-by. May we not seek natural ways, to live supernatural lives.

Lord, teach us to look for Your unseen and invisible realm, where miracles are held waiting for us to live out each day. You let us know, "*Signs, wonders, and miracles follow those who BELIEVE!*"

Let us be found believing, Lord Jesus, walking in Your Glory, taking dominion where there's been loss. Let Your restorative power, be enforced and infused within, as we rise out of the ashes of defeat, and attain the triumph assured us.

Isaiah 58:14

Psalm 29:11

Mark 16:17-18

John 14:27

2 Corinthians 2:14

2 Corinthians 4:8

Galatians 5:1

1 Timothy 6:12

2 Tim 4:7

2 Thessalonians 3:16

Assurance of Victory!

L ord Jesus, You remind us daily, we are Yours and You long to impart assurance of our victory, conveying Your love, exposing us to Your peace.

You gave us the word "THROUGH," affirming there will be a COMING OUT! The floods, fires, and trials we enter into, will not influence our lives, unless we submit to them.

Abraham, while taking Isaac up the mountain to sacrifice him: "He said to his servants, '*Stay here with the donkey while I and the boy go over there. We will worship and then we will come back to You.*'"

Abraham knew they both were coming back down. (Genesis 22:5). He walked with confidence toward Your request to sacrifice his son. He believed, with his entire heart, You had a plan, one that didn't include killing his son Isaac.

Abraham's love and trust in You, revealed it's possible to walk toward Your voice instructing us away from what seems rational, when we cannot see our secure destiny.

As we pursue Your plans over our lives, we're assured that the road we are on is clear, and lit with the light and fire of Your Spirit. Teach us to cultivate the soil of the burdensome places we find ourselves in, and behold, the mysteries promised, bringing richness to our souls.

We shall dig deep, thru the pages of Your word, and solve the mysteries within. May we reach into Your wellspring of liberation, releasing and enabling us to breathe in deeply, the aroma from Your glorious throne.

Let us be found planting Your banners, sharing our sincere love, showing allegiance to our King, our King of Glory. We will display Your authority causing our enemies to languish; for we've built fortresses with the spoils from their assaults.

If we're attacked on one side, You remind us we're hemmed in behind and before, and Your word is our shield. If our adversary sneaks up from behind, You assure us, You're our rear guard.

May we remain strong and stalwart, knowing the moment we said "yes" to You, the YES You spoke over us, stands throughout eternity!

(Gen 22:5)

Isaiah 45:3

Isaiah 52:12

Matthew 13:11

Your kingdom advances!

You say in Your Word, "*The kingdom of God is forcefully advancing and forceful men and women lay hold of it!*"

We ask forgiveness, for allowing doubt and fear into our hearts, causing us to shrink back, withdrawing from the battles, we're meant to face. You beckon us into Your secret place of trust and hope, imparting confidence to accomplish our mission, established before time began.

We declare unification among those in the body of believers, and within the bounds of the buildings we gather in; with one voice, we'll rejoice in You, our Savior.

We declare a merging and melding, becoming one body, expanding Your kingdom on earth, as it is in the heavens.

The religious spirit attempts to blind many to the way of freedom, but no ground is taken, no pacts have been spoken, only truths revealed.

We wrap ourselves in Your armor of light, and ask Your fire to destroy the adversary's plans, trying to invade our lives, communities, and the world. You broke the chains of death and released us into our destinies!

Let no mountain we face, cause us to stagger or fall short of the course You have assigned us. There are no floods or fires that can overtake us, for You promised to bring us through!

Remind us, Lord, we always begin from a place of dominion and triumph, for our futures are secured by Your loving hand! Your kingdom come, and Your will be done, on earth as it is in heaven.

May we step away, and stand aside, from heading in our own direction, and allow You full access to every intricate part and minutiae of our lives. Your way is gloriously filled with Your protection, which looks nothing like our own!

This is the day You have made; we will enter in rejoicing, driving our banners of victory into the ground we've ascended!

Matthew 6:10

Matthew 11:12

Joshua 1:3-7

Isaiah 43:1

Isaiah 51:7

Isaiah 54:4

Psalm 118:24

Psalm 143:9

Revelations 2:26

We are standing on Solid Ground!

J esus, You pick us up and turn us around, and set our feet on solid ground.

You gather those who can't, and show them they can, bringing those who won't, and show them their will.

You surround those alone, and put them together, and You take those together, and make them all one. You hold tears of criers and fill up their deserts, with flocks in their wastelands, create vineyards of wealth.

You lift throngs in sorrow, carrying them to Your light, shifting mourning to joy, reigning all through the night. You transform paths crooked, and straighten their corners, and lower all mountains, for all passersby.

You collect all Your feeble and turn them toward power, speaking courage to the timid, and for the faithful to stand. You bring us to walls, coaching us as we climb, and hand us bronze bows, granting strength while we bend them.

You engage us in battles in our valleys of tears, and train us to stand when retreating for years. You turn our deep valleys into mountains of Glory, and take fearful thoughts, writing us a new story.

You turn anxious days, ones leaving us breathless, ushering in esteemed Presence, chasing darkness away. You take just one life with no plans of doing, and lay out a future for dreadful long days.

You turn those who can't sing, to sensational singers, and then take those singers, and make them Your Choir. You give new songs, for all days of old ones, and take those who won't dance, and teach them they can. You gather Your instruments and build a great orchestra, taking many new players, giving them Your new heart!

You take ones who worship, up mountains of hardship, and bring them back down, as warriors over darkness. You created all strategies for current-day battles, showing servants their threshold, training them how to soar.

You transform all Your children, making them into champions, and take all Your champions, winning battles against conflict! We all stand victorious, children reigning for our King, keeping restful assurance, while tucked under Your Wing.

Mark 7:24-27

1 Corinthians 1:10

Isaiah 43:19

Psalm 18:34

Psalm 40:31

Psalm 63:1

Jeremiah 31

Isaiah 65:21

Revelation 3:21

Courage Imparted

Lord Jesus, we invite You to take us into places we're reluctant to enter, facing any fears, leaving fully charged, infused with courage.

If we confront a spirit of death, we'll be excited to push back with Your Spirit of life, and when we encounter terror, we'll be thrilled with our new-found faith!

Lord, we yearn to face all impossibilities, while eagerly waiting to experience them bending their knees to the possibilities of our unrelenting faith! We'll long to face all the, "You cannot do's," spoken to us, so we'll consistently live in the hope that we CAN!

When we meet discouragement and depression, we will not be overcome by it; instead, we're excited to bring our praise and thanksgiving, which imparts our much-welcomed COURAGE!!

When we meet true darkness, we'll be passionate, displaying Your authentic and true light! We'll face and confront them all and find great faith, but the greatest of all will be Your abiding love, Lord Jesus!

We've found the amazing grace and light of You, Lord, where true love exists. You are our Wonderful, Counselor, great I Am, Everlasting Father, Prince of Peace, and Lord of Lords!! We will live sheltered in the great Name of Jesus!!

Isaiah 29:18

Psalm 107:14

Hosea 13:14

Matthew 19:26

Mark 9:2

Mark 10:27

Luke 1:37

John 1:9

John 3:21

1 Corinthians 15:55

2 Corinthians 4:6

Ephesians 5:9

Revelation 12:11

In such a time as this!

Lord, in such a time as this, You call us to a deeper place, one with increased intimacy, where fear no longer grips us, and Your peace invades our soul.

In this secret place, we'll find Your voice is clearer and Your sweet fragrance overwhelms us. Lord, Your touch, more tangible, while we experience Your presence lifting the weight of burdens.

May we dare to walk toward Your voice, calling out to us, *"Come away with Me, from all that hinders you; from all that prevents you from entering into My sanctuary of safety."*

We consistently find Your hand, signaling us to come closer, inviting us in to our destiny! We feel the floor of heaven tremble, while Your voice awakens our spirits when inviting us into Your chambers.

Our chest pounds with excitement; because we've made a choice to leave behind the ordinary and predictable, journeying toward new beginnings and unseen realms of Your glory!

May we be like David, who ran toward Goliath, without distress, while the men of war frantically ran away in terror and panic.

Let us we as Esther, who willingly and courageously approached the king, knowing she could perish, but risked it all to save her people from destruction. Lord, find us brave and bold, for we know You've called us into a safe place, hidden under the shadow of Your wings.

This place, unfamiliar and mysterious to many, but for those who answer Your invitation, we'll never be the same. We shall be captured; captivated by Your love and transformed by Your matchless power.

Because of Your great grace, we are equipped to be released, bringing much-needed change to the world within us and around us.

Esther 5:2

Psalm 81:7

Psalm 91:1-16

Daniel 2:37

Marl 6:7

Luke 9:2

Luke 19:38

Romans 12:2

2 Corinthians 3:18

We will rise while we wait!

Jesus, Your timing is impeccable and flawless; we are blessed when we wait on You. Forgive us, Lord, if You find us drumming our fingers or questioning Your ability.

May You find us yielded and praising You, while we remain in a posture of expectancy. We will stand aside, allowing Your management of our time; for we trust Your perfected plans do exist in Your Kingdom.

Find us, Lord, eagerly abiding in Your word, for we know Your goodness has gone on before us. We come with childlike confidence in our Father's intention over lives. We give You permission to march ahead of us, shoring up Your plans that pertain to life's details.

You've written the books of our lives, those numbered days, with moments captured by Your heavenly camera. Each day, a page is made, and at its end, folded and into the next.

As we make our trek through, we are thankful for the assurance of Your faithfulness and love. We'll reflect on days we felt overwhelmed; remembering You didn't leave us, and You never will.

Our weakness is, indeed, a place of empowerment and meekness before You, Lord; it creates in us a fruitful branch. Swing wide Your heavenly gates and release us, from all that's held us captive.

We call peace, to flow like a raging river after a torrential rainstorm. Fill the places, which were parched by endless days, spent without hope and weariness from sleepless nights.

We will dance a celebratory dance, one that signifies our victory and lay to rest our feeble beliefs and doubt-filled days.

As we turn the page of time, we'll make a firm stance, holding a victory banner with our left and faith's shield on our right.

Lamentations 3:23

1 Samuel 18:6

2 Samuel 6:14

Isaiah 30:18

Psalm 3:8

Psalm 27:14

Psalm 42:5

Psalm 56:41

Psalm 89:2

Peter 1:23

Blessed by not seeing

Believing and not seeing, brings blessings into our lives, for Your word declares, *"Blessed are those who have not seen and yet believe."*

We long to please You, Jesus, and by faith, we're given a seed, and encouraged to grow it. Our faith seed has potential to move mountains, and it lays within the tilled soil of humility.

Hope has substance, and our sight is not required to enter Your pleasure. How we begin has much to do with the way we finish, and the way we finish has most to do, with offering thanks in dark days and sleepless nights.

The floods and fires of Your word remind us, we'll not be harmed by the flames and frigid cold waters of adversity. Since Your word is a shield around us, we'll feel secure, comforted through our valleys with shadows of death.

Our sometimes-lonely path has provision from Your throne. You are our Need-meeter and Supplier on our journey, laid out before time began.

You beckon us to the deep waters of trust, pulling out the moon and stars, reminding us how limited we are. We may not see You, but we hear Your voice calling us away from the ankle-deep waters we've found ourselves standing.

We see the wind, whipping up calm waters, attempting to stir panic, but we come in spite of what's seen, because we know You sent us.

You rend the darkness, revealing the light needed to shine on our way through the turbulent seas of doubt. You're our Beginning and our End, our Light and the Love of our lives.

As the Author of the books of life, may it be penned within each page, "*Through the momentary light afflictions, we stayed the course and we finished the race gracefully, not fixing our eyes on what is seen, but the invisible, powerful King of kings, and Lord of lords!*"

Proverbs 4:18

Psalm 8:3

Psalm 84:5

Psalm 119:1

Psalm 119:105

Matthew 5:6

Matthew 5:10

John 20:29

2 Corinthians 4:17

In Closing

I recall a time in my life as a small girl when I was taken over by fear.

I was standing at the shoreline of the ocean, while the tide was low, watching my parents wander further out, while clam digging.

I was holding their bucket, as they dug up the yummy clams, wondering how many more they would place in my container because it was getting heavy.

As little waves rolled in, lapping over my tiny feet, I was caught off guard by a much bigger one.

The small ripple turned into a powerful surge, and as the water receded, the sand beneath my feet washed away, leaving me alarmed.

I panicked, as the sand I was solidly standing on, was gone, and I could not regain my footing.

My once secure place was lost, and I dropped the bucket, half filled with clams!

I was mortified as I watched all my treasured clams spill out of the bucket, and float away.

I remember my father screaming at me, as he watched all the clams lost in the waves, while I felt the water getting deeper.

I ran toward the shore with my empty bucket, back to safety, watching my parents attempt to gather all the clams, scattered throughout the water.

Many years later, as an adult, there have been times I've felt the same panic, as the once secure place I had been standing, seemingly washed away.

God lets us know in his Word... Psalm 18:2 (NIV) "The Lord is my rock, my fortress, and my deliverer; my God is my rock, in whom I take refuge, my shield and the horn of my salvation, my stronghold."

Psalm 62:2 (NIV) "Truly he is my rock and my salvation; he is my fortress, I will never be shaken."

Psalm 62:6 (NIV) "He only is my rock, and my salvation; he is my defense; I shall not be moved."

For me, the most secure place is standing on God's solid ground, which is Christ and His Word.

He reminds us that any ground other ground than Him is not reliable.

The words in this book have been given and continue to be imparted to me by the Lord.

While I sit listening...waiting for heaven to deposit its transforming words, they seem to wrap around me like a soft blanket.

I remain still, waiting to release onto paper what God places on the tablets of my heart.

With readied hands, I write what I hear Jesus share, eager to be lifted up in my spirit, saturated in the rich fullness of His comforting invitation to His secret place.

When I share these powerful words with others, they too are touched and released from what troubled their soul, declaring it is well once again.

Some have written to me, letting me know their once-troubled spirits were set free by God's calming, comforting words.

I believe as you read these prayers, you'll feel a sense of closeness with Jesus.

If you once felt distant from Him, you will experience the lifting of burdens from these anointed words.

When you're in life's storms; causing the fortress around you to shake from the winds of adversity, you will be empowered by God's kindness and love toward you.

If you have any questions or comments, I invite you to write. Classycalves@gmail.com

May God richly bless you, Sherrie

Author Biography-

Sherrie Brown above all is a 'Child of God' who has been leading and discipling many out of their strongholds for over 25 years.

She walked away from an emotionally charged childhood and with courage, she faced the haunting of her past. Now healed, Sherrie leads others into their promised land, cheering them on to their victory.

She is a Visioneer and inventor, having attained three (3) U.S. Design Patents on Leg Wear, and is the owner of Classy Calves™ She is also a former Hair Salon owner.

Sherrie is a wife, mother and an-up-and coming author and speaker, who loves to spend time on her family's boat, in the vast waters of the Puget Sound.

Her passion is ministering inner healing and deliverance to women, sharing key revelations for overcoming obstacles which stop many at the door of their destiny.

" My degree of willingness, to relinquish every part of my life to Jesus, is the degree of His benefits, I'll freely receive." ~ Sherrie Brown

Made in the USA
San Bernardino, CA
18 December 2019